Foxy Love

All-American Poems

Foxy Love

All-American Poems

by

Matt Thomas

Cover image photo of AIDS Memorial Quilt
courtesy of the National AIDS Memorial
Author photo by Michelle Thomas

ISBN: 979-8-90146-715-2
Library of Congress Control Number: 2026931909

Kelsay Books
502 South 1040 East, A-119
American Fork, Utah 84003
Kelsaybooks.com

Acknowledgments

The following poems were previously published

The Ablanatha Review: "San Bernardino"
The Big Windows Review: "I Know That My Redeemer Liveth"
High Horse: "Friday Night, Tascosa"
The Insurgence: "Crown City"
North of Oxford: "Summer Blood"
Slab Magazine: "J"
Streur Nature Anthology (North of Oxford, 2025): "Pause"
Temz Review: "Drunk and Disorderly"
The Penwood Review: "The Divine Scales"
Ponder Review: "While on Leave"
River Heron Review: "Fishing the Conemaugh"

Thank you to my family, my 'home country.' Thank you to my neighbors at home in Virginia and in DC, Northern Michigan, Pennsylvania, and especially Southern California, where the idea for this book took shape and the poems "San Bernardino" and "Crown City (All-American)" were written.

Thank you to the National AIDS Memorial for their work and use of their image of the AIDS Memorial Quilt. Thank you to the many Americans who reached out to me via social media this year, and to the millions of people working diligently for peace, inclusion, equity, science, and betterment in every corner of our country and the world every day.

Contents

San Bernardino

We lost a dog, a mule, and a horse within the space of a month

Weird expression, within the space of,
thoughts keeping time, another one, less strange
more practical while hiking, trying and failing
to be in the moment, a crow following me like an itchy cough,
shadow swinging front to back. Touching each Ponderosa
like expensive showroom furniture, self-conscious,
replaying the book I read while resting at lunch in which

a characters asks
how winter ducks know that paddling around
will keep their water ice free. What instinct? Pining
after the idea that there is stratified sense in us,
a natural how-to,
like the assumption of a terrible god,
disguised as mundane to save our eyes
maybe come to earth as a duck,
taking its turn to swim an ice-free circle,
or a 500-year-old tree unable to avert eyes from
our common sense,
heavy in the mountains burned at the bottom
and freshly ancient on their fogged tops

Ages ago, as my grandmother used to say

Although ages actually have passed:
youth, early adulthood, our 40s. You were dropping me off,
morning after
and were running late.

I had up until then never thought to “keep” time;
I didn’t know that I could care about it.
But you said, look, catching my eye
while I tried to think of something to say to keep you, look,
I’m not trying to be a dick but you have to get out, I’m *late,*
the word emphasized like a gust
in a tree, and you shooed me,
with your hands, a silly thought, out onto the curb,
and drove off while I was still talking.
No one had ever dismissed me with such raw authority
and I thought now that
is a person with skills to poach.
Just this morning I dropped you off
at your office and remembering that incident 30 years ago
I was instinctually careful
to allow you the trait of punctuality.

Two characters visit
a sculpture of an angel in a garden
and to the one it’s frightening;
she can’t tell if it’s a man or woman, robed and kneeling
in a feminine way but broad chinned and big knuckled.
She feels she is being asked to believe in something catholic
her phrase
for the expression of a zoo gorilla surveying
what must/cannot possibly be
his domain phrased as ‘something catholic,’
fussed with angle brackets and shims,
temporary shelf lived fixes for fundamental problems.

The wavering border
between what ‘must be’ and what is painful
to look at, a crack descending into the bottom of the world or
angels and god laid flat, in intervals a few inches
beyond stride length
so that you have to make an effort
to ascend: stairs, nature’s fundamental symbol
that there is a way up and out. Not to get closer to something,
rather to expend a time;
a series of pragmatic dismissals and possessions,
interruptions asking

that we accede to season;
a rough stone thought, chinned and knuckled with the presumption
that the present is for nothing but the future

fearful and true, as I thought how much simpler
chores have been, life in general, minus the dog, mule, and horse
in the pause while their replacements,
fixing sap trembling from a pinecone prickle waiting
to undream, crystalize into a dirt path, foot-rubbed rock,
an instinctual glance at my watch, swig from bottle
stumbling, dripping water down the front of my shirt,
stains resembling maps of distant needs,
comforts and fears received, from and to,
little pains and alarms in the joints of things.

Flag Raising

Unpacked
from folded custom

a rat beneath the holly
pink dry babies in the mulch

cars gassing by, revving between blocks
snow in the forecast

roaches thick and dumb in the cold

space heaters plugged in, blowing,
jackets hung behind doors

My country, secured
top and bottom

to kite the wind,
inching upward

above steaming breath, sewers,
eyes flashing border signals

while we watch, chin aspired
to the ritual of arriving

on our own immigrant shores

At the Movies

Who is holding hands, conversing
with whom is of no consequence,
all of us stoppered, lone late-night readers
beside the knock and thump
of a party next door considering
math, the toolbox of difference,
each sensible purpose rotated
to a season of zero. Board the ship,
plane, yoke the oxen,
bombard yourself with gamma rays
just be careful to arrive
before the lights go down, avoid the sight
of popcorn, Skittles,
dark sticky puddles of Pepsi,
all the cheap hard lived bits
threatening suspension
with the prejudice of the past.
Catastrophic breaches do occur, have, recently,
everyone commingling,
running through each other's fingers
no matter the junctions or timeline of origin,
disappointing the neat outcome
of each consciousness seeking its own layer
in the known density of story, memory, and hope,
peer reviewed thumbs up interference-free stimuli
worth a vertiginous stumble walking
the impossibly flat hallway out

toward the knit of familiar knowns,
pink tinged tissue of hour standing
for the whole of the day.

I Know That My Redeemer Liveth

The hour is announced short,

Westminster Chimes missing
a middling B, ringing

in our heads, remembered,
duller, less loud,
than the struck G, F, and E

No one is fashionable today.
The count comes in too soon,
off-beat; vanities burn
out of time, in the difference,

smoke

the color of lungs
drying, sucking
raw air between buildings,

history breach born

before the first chime
of the series on a fixed scale
of what must be noon.

The Dream

after Rousseau

Whoever buys this house after we leave it will cut the trees back,
I'm certain. It's always been unseemly in suburban America
to allow nature to cat up against you
in the way that we do but we fell in love over
a shared inability to subvert ourselves
to the opinions of others so, as is our motto, fuck 'em.

I'm writing this on the sundeck in a gale,
beneath waving widowmakers tempting
what morbidity and mortality statisticians call
'accidental tree failure,' a phrase that perfectly captures
everything that people don't understand about nature.

Our realtor thought the couple who built our house suspect,
meaning that they shared our insistence to diverge from typical.
They carved a crooked heart into the lintel,
created too many windows,
refused the traditional aesthetic borders:
choices that drove their banker to distraction, sure
that the house would not sell
yet it did, to us, compatriots of the weird.

It’s a cold March that’s blowing, trying to husband the sun
warming me unconcerned
with how its reach is received, same as the plants pushing up
through frost in the shade that will soon cause a riot
of line trimming and lawn mowing. I want you out here,
naked, the two of us waiting
for our yard to clothe us in contrast, sprout
the eyes of lions and monkeys, birds from books.

There are people who have a secret gripe against life
but thank God that’s not us. We live our complaint, failing
accidentally on friends and families, sometimes each other,
a tasty speculative risk considering
that self-realization occurs in the weeds, free
to those unashamed of their hunger.

Foxy Love

Yipping of pups,
unknown things
squealing at the silence
of the earth, a quiet not
without consequence,
floored with bones,
trash

Me and you
and the stolen contents of our hearts

that's foxy love
curled up,
S's in a tight space,
sharpening each other's keen sense
of the past littering
a full bellied present.

Fishing the Conemaugh

An Ode to the Johnstown Flood

Just another boasting playmate
until it swore and rose

having absorbed the support
of the beaded grasses,
dripping cedars,
boated catalpa

bulged,
feeling a discovered violence

when yesterday
the worst it could do was leeches

became aimless, terrifying to itself
spewing frogs, snakes, wasps.

Not the contour of the land itself,
(scraped into a pinch)
or variation of its usage
(woods trespassing the old abutment)

but the way that one such each
is lined or shaded by a branch
and those too scratched by others
the nearer it becomes.

And the haze
of bared blue beneath the clouds:

a thoughtful poverty of detail
implying plenty,
lifted as a consequence
of the canopy to a constant,

scat of an extinct
furnaced progress aligning
to legends

once rendered as living wills,
uninhabited now,
free to reclaim, remake
in the image of a new thirst.

Cast and it’s the dead,
          not fish, that rise
migrant still, unwilling
to let go that new consideration
          made
by miracle of engineering
on the biblical sand.

Hoops, balls, hearthstones,
barrows, thread, buttons:
crafted expectations mass graved
where once stored for safe keeping;

the detritus of a folk
fed the American appetence,

a parallel country
compressing beneath history,
fuel turning to fuel.

Allegheny, Little Otter, Stony Creek:
a confluence emptying the present
into the past, but passing through,
as if in hand, those ghosts

who unconveyed sweat,
a milling fog skeining the water,
no stomach for the air.

Deer Tick

A singular itch
defined by intervals, legs
landing in a sequence
initiating the shape
of an O, nail to nail
to pinch it from your skin,
hold it moving
like a wound thing
before dropping it into the sink
to circle and disappear
into the dark hole that you watch,
while running water
until certain
it has drowned in the trap,
a long way
as is said
from your heart

While on Leave

Your breath catching
as the car lurched and stalled.
The pedals fat and cool
beneath your bare feet.
The ball of the shifter snug in your palm
and his hand warm on top of yours
while the gnarled hickories spun
across the bug-stained windshield.
He moved your hand through the gears,
brother,
the bones
of his skinny arm against your own
as you leaned on the tightly closed mouth of each gear
until it yielded deliciously slow,
the grease still morning-cold and thick.

He is instructing you,
holding his cigarette out the window with one hand and
gesturing inside of the car with his other.
You toss your head as you listen, then
push your hair back behind your ears with both hands,
dragging your fingers slowly down to your jawbone
as is your habit.

There's a bee on the windowsill.
And off somewhere a Catbird is cawing.
You wish for one daydream
in the here and now
instead of stuff gone off, ashed
from the day drawn down
into your own, retreating, wake.

Moccasins

I've been tracking my insides around,
same as a toad's one pointed toe hashes
his trail in the mud,

the little cellular walls of which
flatten into the larger wetness
that floats yellow moccasins

luck launched at a slip
of variegated wale, empty and usual
without the delicate little bowls

riding circumstance beneath
an emerging sun winning the day
in slow and steady ascent

up the appropriately named
fire road east to west,
the closest thing to God

on earth, while we,
not even minor deities
of this world or any,

less perfect than a flower boat,
go about our perpetual, awkward
teenage depredations amazed

at our hormonal confusion,
bleeding on the tracks
of our travels, existing

in this form on the way to another,
covering ground,
calling that progress.

Wim Hoff

Hyperventilating yourself

to restore peace
as if an original condition.

Up in our trees, we've never seen
the forest. In the bush never

experienced the thicket.
Imagine a fire in your belly.

Imagine that you are feeding the fire.
Truly experience

Wednesday night dinner
across from your life partner,

a mind-blowing descriptor when
(if only you could really)

think about it

Nesting Impulse

The day starts with a squawk, mewl,
ends in a bark at shadows
passing on tiny hooves down
a murmuration of trails
you have to squint to see,
a promising tangle
of bare raspberry bushes in April
not obligated to July,
framed in memory signifying
an artifact, asking
for analysis, critical comparison
to other days such as this one,

lumbering jets invisible but for the outline
landing at Reagan in a fog
like whales descending strata of slush,
wingless birds, real
as dinosaurs feathered from rocks,
or my office three miles away brooding
architectural assumption: two

of my many worlds existing
apart from touch, in theory and math,
like the duck that nests yearly in a flower box
outside the Peet's Coffee on 17th,
perpetually there and not, now
a bowled, empty mash of sticks
bearing the impression of her body
the way that a bite betrays
a head and a mouth, or

the referenced horizontal
of my imagined progress implies
the azimuth of my destination; maybe
the smooth, familiar
shape of yesterday's arrival.

Dim Sum

The phoenix claws

always remind me

of how you once a day ask

do I feel hot?

and move your forehead toward me

to wait for the back of my hand,

the barest meat over bone,

fat with ceremony,

if not luck

Drunk and Disorderly

Grimy as the plywood inside of a box car
Something in the squelch
of those other stories
People small inside themselves,
riding along in the institutional smell
watching the bouncing ponytail jutting
from the back of a brown Snapback
tied in faded yellow elastic.

I'm guessing Iraq or Afghanistan,
that

familiarity is a relief just past the scratch
for both of us,

our homes waiting, same
lights on, about the business of any separate space
while we occupy this one,
a Dodge Charger Pursuit
courtesy of, like everything since,
9/11
those microplastics sweating from everything,

air of recalcitrant critical knowledge
          bordering life and death,
suspicion
that anything benign is left of bang.

Which is why we're riding in a silent,
studious avoidance of conversation,
you driving as if clearing a house,
shirt bulging slightly above your duty belt.
A soft thing
like me deployed to boredom and fear,
a polyester heart
beating in the Kevlar,

engaging by not,
my sister,
the two of us safely within
the predictable outcomes
of Standard Operating Procedure.

Ode to Our Security

A rotation of guards in the lobby, dissimilar in appearance
but same focus on intense, day long phone calls
as if along with marksmanship and self-defense
they are each required to master passing through
and out of time, leaving a magnetic trace,
snaking, tonguing words in the vehicular breeze
of our back and forth between
offices and the lobby, elevators, restrooms,
wound back with sucked teeth and a pencil while
day passes and it becomes increasingly awkward to walk by;
you've said good morning, hi, nodded, smiled
so now find the corners of the room, anywhere
but the desk where they sit
on overwatch Facetiming while
prepared to outwit the whims of our tensions
in tactical gray and black,
ugly sneakers misshapen by the weight of waiting,
blocky overlarge handguns
tugging at waistlines even
the flag wears ashes ignoring both form and function
to spite beauty, the new enemy of the people, yet
there it is, in a look up
from a phone assessing the threat of you,
risk of breach
to our busy, sunny valley
where we are rippling grass, shimmering water,

and in that slow look, like that of a shaggy cow,
there are all the stunning questions of species,
domesticated creatures
observing each other between
paddocks and uses,
and a comment on consciousness, similar
to the way that lead skies
reveal the contours of the land.

Biomimetics

If we discovered running water
we built a dam
spending most of the day
cartoon engineers
running from one breach to the next
remaking the world

The drying bed
snaked in the sun leaving
its curled algae edge
like a flaking skin
waiting for the nimble memory,
a day or two,
to recall its habit,
work the knot we tied

so that returning we found
a muddy surge flooding
our efforts re-engineered
as an amber'd intuition that affect
is familiarity
is accomplishment

similar

to how stepping over magnolia petals
storm smeared on the flagstones
in the flowering light of the courtyard weakens
my knees in the elevator
this morning recalling

the hair tied loosely back
on your head, love
for the mussed intimate
as proportion, beauty,

ruin

of the blueprints, win
for our persistent, sacred elements
expressing the happiness
of their will

Friday Night, Tascosa

For Chelle

Not like the killers
spitting into Whataburger cups,
emptying themselves trying
to be hard as the land,
you keep a word
between lip and gum
and swallow your spit,
saving yourself for the moment
when the ponytails swishing
from the backs of baseball caps
stomp down from the bleachers
in a Great Migration
to join legs and necks waiting
beyond the stadium pawing
the black Llano stretching
away from boys snorting
under lights to a freedom
with nothing to prove.

Pause

Stopped on the bridge
the dog and I
to watch plumed wood ducks
script their intentions
in the thin ice of the backwater

On the opposite bank
a heron stands curled into the weather
waiting it out

Back at the farm I'd paused
to piss in the bushes,
every chore hassling my insides
even urination no escape
from closing doors
on each named, evil thing.
I reached to touch a cedar branch
thumb and forefinger on the green

soft mature leaves learned
to relax,
not spiky itching like the young
begging for calm,
invasive as it,
another noxious weed pushing, existing
for its own enlightenment.

Frogs
deep in mud measure
lengthening light

as the diesel idles and ticks,
each noisy stroke predicting
the space before the next

Each of us reining
at our own clock,
equivalence existing
in the quiet not
the croaking

Summer Blood

The road gradually narrows,
swells and crowns from the flat of winter,
yellow lines fattening, acquiring texture.

Lifted onto the shoulders
of kudzu, creeper, honeysuckle,
draped snake back and stomach
over bump and hollow,
mica scales emerging from the asphalt,
oil in the pores slicking the rain:

summer blood poking what had crawled
into sun to sleep to quicken
through beer cans and 4-barrel carburetors,
condoms and classic metal,
fast food bags flowering in the bar ditch.

I stopped this morning
to lift a box turtle across that road
neck giraffed and on its toes
in dark relief against the shaking green.
I've seen the hardest people do the same;
brake suddenly, activate hazards
and door jutting into the middle of a two lane,
stoop to carry old, cold blood
to where it wants to go.

J

He walks to the window and asks, Do you see him?
as if of the street streaming between root waked curbs
and nods, to his reflection maybe or to the weather,
noting a shadow detach from a lamp post,
flit to another and merge
into the trunk of a rain whipped hornbeam.
He struggles into a jacket and swiping his keys
from an ash tray descends
the metal steps of the fire escape to the street,
the iron pegs knocking in their sockets,
sending mortar into the gusty wind.

New boots, hands in pockets, affecting nonchalance,
he walks hunched against the rain
past that particular tree feeling a presence
and makes the signal, like playing spies.
He recognizes his Hyundai, a dark lump
smeared with watery streetlight at the curb
and walks to it, opens the door, sits.
He fidgets and waits, making an exercise of
refusing the urge to chastise himself
until the wind blows suddenly into the car
as the passenger door is flung open
and the young man, boy, he thinks,
drops into the seat, blooming cigarette smoke,
body odor and wet jeans.

They exchange a quick glance and then
he leans out of the way while
the other unbuckles, threads his fly
with cold and clammy fingers,
coaxes his suddenly reluctant blood
to pool slowly into his belly and
when the seduction is achieved
he relaxes, consoled, his left boot finding
the pleasant resistance of the dead pedal
and watches the back of the other's head,
trucker cap logo too worn to read,
a bit of pollen from the hornbeams caught
at the nape of his neck. A pause and

"No touching bro," when he removes it.

At the same point as always he blurts,
despite himself,
so softly that he can hardly feel the words,
"Say my name,"
and immediately humiliated, says again,
"forget it, forget it,"
and swaps the person of the other, his heat
and hair and smell and sound,
for an old mental standby,
a dog-eared cardboard thing

and after a time is able
to loose himself into the night,
and the rain, and Spring, and the hornbeams.
Then reaches, with no tactile means
toward the rustle of clothes as the other sits up,
takes the damp, crumpled twenty from the cup holder
and opens the door to the elements.

When the door closes
into what he knows is a very sacred kind of silence he sits,
breathing, slowing his heart and then
opens his own door
and high steps toward the sidewalk shallows
creating a wake against the current; ungainly and imperfect.

Watching from the window,
he's a dirty white smear on the blue-black ribbon,
a swimmer, knocking the river from his ears with a hand
striding away, having endured his moment
under the hip of nature and emerged
into air that is for that instant caressing, not buffeting,
conversing,
the voice of it carrying bell-clear over the water.

The Divine Scales

I hadn't seen the usual attendant for weeks
and so asked the new old boy, 'Did he quit?'
'His heart did,' is what he said,
pushing at a broom.

He had been a horrible racist, but kind to me
a fellow white rural man,
asking after my father,
telling me, 'I'll bring him up to prayer group.'

I'm tempted to imagine an eternal reckoning
but prefer to think
that his meanness simply died with him
and his kindness too,

more now of both in the world
to weight the discrimination between values
never so opposite
as to conveniently balance.

Crown City (All-American)

The type of beach town that I was raised to love
but knew was not for my kind of white privilege:
waxed wake boards like teak Chris-Craft runabouts,
oxford shirts and Vans.
A jacked-up golf cart, chrome wheels, stereo,
four or five teenage boys, you know,
tow headed, t-shirted,
bubbled wrapped in the kind of comfortable
that they assume they will always be,
eternals, lower gods at least of America,
actually not least, you can say a lot about America but not that.
Tan golden haired limbs waving to a hip hop beat,
screeching silly boys that still make me jealous;
though I leveled up with their parents I'll never get
to be a teenage hero. Walked past thinking these thoughts
when I heard a crash,
plastic breaking, metal scraping concrete
and looking back over my shoulder saw the cart on its side,
still blasting the SoundCloud rapper,
the boys tangled in the roll cage like clout gold,
their mothers forced to spin summers
in beach cottages by Uncle Sam at flag point.
And did I think of them then as trapped, maybe
no more satisfied than me despite the glimmer? Did I
return to help? I did not,

I walked to lunch at an outdoor table down the street,
to the hollow plonk of a gold card acquired too late,
a tanned all-American high school,
tennis braceleted waitress I never got to date,
left that mess to their all-American dads,
to gather round in their permanent golf beer buzz and figure out.
I ate the overpriced sandwich I can afford now
looking steadily in the opposite direction,
thinking a hearty fuck all y'all,
and me, too,
for still wanting in, tangled up sideways,
to have those kinds of scars,
the kind that guarantee a great remember when,
a cost-free laugh: ease made from ease taken.

About the Author

Matt Thomas is a smallholder farmer, engineer, and poet. *Foxy Love: All-American Poems* is his third collection. His first, *Disappearing by the Math,* was published in 2024 by Silver Bow. A second full-length collection, *Cicada, Dog & Song,* will be published by Serving House Books in 2026.

His poetry has appeared in *Triggerfish Critical Review, Ponder Review, Hampden-Sydney Review, Hiram Review, Dunes Review, Avalon Literary Review, Galway Review, Milk House Review, Cleaver Magazine, River Heron Review, The Thieving Magpie, Common House Magazine, Slab Magazine, The Broken Plate, Spellbinder Magazine, Pinhole Poetry, Susurrus Magazine, Temz Review,* and elsewhere.

He and his family live in Virginia where they practice land conservation and stewardship in the historic Shenandoah Valley. They are glad denizens of D.C., Philadelphia, Traverse City, Marquette, and San Diego.

Website:
www.mattthomaspoetry.com

Threads and Instagram:
@mattthomaspoetry

www.ingramcontent.com/pod-product-compliance
Lightning Source LLC
LaVergne TN
LVHW050611100826
845148LV00015B/3221

9798901467152